Speak Camfranglais pour un Renouveau Ongolais

Peter Wuteh Vakunta

Langaa Research & Publishing CIG
Mankon, Bamenda

Publisher
Langaa RPCIG
Langaa Research & Publishing Common Initiative Group
P.O. Box 902 Mankon
Bamenda
North West Region
Cameroon
Langaagrp@gmail.com
www.langaa-rpcig.net

Distributed in and outside N. America by African Books Collective
orders@africanbookscollective.com
www.africanbookcollective.com

ISBN: 9956-791-76-8

DISCLAIMER
All views expressed in this publication are those of the author and do not necessarily reflect the views of Langaa RPCIG.

Dédicace

A Ali Baba et ses quarante feymams
séjournant sur le sol ongolais

Table des Matières

Avant-propos...v

Apprenti-sorcier..1

Je wanda..2

Shiba..4

Manioc..6

Massa Inoni...8

Ashawo man pikin...10

Al-Qaeda..11

Grand Camarade..12

Pont de Wouri..14

Chairman..16

Français mboko...17

Mami Wata...18

Bagdad...20

Ndamba...22

Bakassi...24

Sonara..25

Affaire Anglo...26

Ngataman (Hommage à Lapiro).................................27

Homme-Lion...28

Méga-tombe d'après Valsero...................................30

Zangalewa... 32

Gombistes... 33

Palais d'Etoudi à D.C..35

Docta..36

A tout casser Camtok.....................................38

Deuxième bureau..................................40

A malin malin et demi.............................. 43

Mini-mignonne...............................46

Speak camfranglais pour un renouveau ongolais......... 50

Schizophrénie nationale............................. 53

Bitter Kola.. 55

A la manière des saras............................ 56

Hymne camerien................................ 57

Glossaire...................................... 65

Avant Propos

La situation socio-linguistique de la République du cameroun a favorisé l'émergence d'un parler jeune—le camfranglais. Qu'est-ce que c'est que le camfranglais ? Il s'agit d'une langue de communication de la jeunesse camerounaise, et plus particulièrement des lycéens et des étudiants universitaires. Sur le plan morphosyntaxique, le camfrangalis se définit comme une langue hybride érigée sur une structure syntaxique et un fond lexical français, de l'emploi des mots empruntés à l'anglais, au pidgin English et aux langues vernaculaires camerounaises. Les locuteurs définissent le camfranglais comme une création camerounaise, voire une déformation du français hexagonal.

Le camfranglais ne bénéficie pas encore d'une étiquette figée. Plusieurs nominations sont employées, avec des occurrences variables—francanglais, francamanglais, fran-anglais, francam, cam-anglais, etc. Toutefois, il convient de souligner le fait que l'emploi du camfranglais se généralise par le temps qui court au Cameroun. Autrement dit, il ne s'agit plus d'une langue strictement des adolescents, puisque les adultes s'en servent à bon escient. En d'autres mots, même si le camfranglais apparaît comme une variété générationnelle (un parler des jeunes), la restriction de sa population n'occulte pas une possible diffusion auprès d'une population plus âgée.

Ce constat nous amène à nous pencher sur une question de taille, à savoir pourquoi écrire en camfranglais ? D'un point de vue global, il faudrait signaler le fait que l'UNESCO vient de conférer au camfranglais la reconnaissance de son statut comme langue à part entière (Cf. *The Study Groups and Literacy Program* de l'UNESCO). Cette reconnaissance place le camfranglais sur un pied d'égalité avec des milliers d'autres langues parlées sur la planète terre. Sur le plan domestique, certains écrivains chevronnés d'origine camerounaise à l'instar de Patrice Nganang, Mercédès Fouda, et Gabriel Kuitche Fonkou se servent déjà du camfranglais comme mode d'écriture littéraire. Pour ceux-ci, le camfranglais symbolise un libre choix qui s'inscrit sans le plurilinguisme ambient camerounais. D'autres voient dans le camfranglais le parler qui pourrait caractériser le français proprement camerounais (Harter, 2005). Sur ce, j'invite le lectorat à se régaler de ma versification du nouveau-né camerounais qu'est le camfranglais.

Aprenti-Sorcier

Dommage à tous ces bouc-émissaires!
Dommage surtout à Hamidou Marafa,
Ce Bao qui est fall du pouvoir
Quand ce djimtété est come au pouvoir depuis from
On lui avait tok que lookot Popol,

Because quand vous n'êtes plus
Dans les good books de l'Homme Lion,
Il risque de vous foutre that coup de tête
Qu'il avait sissia to Eric Chinje.
Lors de l'interview infâme.

But Marafa avait refusé carrément de nous ya.
Il nous avait seulement answer que:
Capos, that wuna own langua na daso allô.
Alors, le voilà aujourd'hui dans la taule inside Kondengui.
Every day, il ne cesse de crier, wohoo! Wohoo!

Popo me I di askam say hein,
Wusai ndiba go commot for come move
Hamido Marafa for that Kondengui fire?
Mbombo, tell me: Qui a raison?
Just now qui est le vrai mboutman?

Est-c'est nous ou c'est Hamido Marafa?
A vous de juger!
Some Aboki don nyè dis palava,
Sotai il a dit seuelment que
A malin malin et demi!

1

Je Wanda

Il y a quelque chose que
Je wanda depuis from,
If par hazard, I say par hasard
Because le locataire d'Etoudi
Ne croit aucunément in the truth of this dictum:
"From dust you came, and to dust you shall return."

Anyhow, si le mandat de Paul Biya parvient à bolè today
That be say, il crève bon gré mal gré,
Who will take his place as père de la nation?
Je wanda seulement et je sabi que
Beaucoup de camers wanda comme moi.
Est-que je dis vrai ou non?

Don't forget that la relève ne
Se prépare pas au Cameroun, hein.
Si Biya crève today, certainement que
Son mandat va bolè un jour, fais quoi fait quoi,
Est-ce que na that garçon de courses
Que vous appelez Cavayé Yéguié Djibril,

Rejeton des parents kirdi from Mada
In the Mayo Sara arrondissement,
Na yi go chop chia ou alors
C'est le soi-disant président du Sénat fantôme
That does not exist qui va squatter à Etoudi
Until further notice, Je wanda seulement?

De toutes les facons, we no wan
See zangalewa for Etoudi si

Popol parvient à crever for better or for worse!
Ongola mérite mieux que les zangalewa half-book
Dem go come nous foutre le bordel
Partout dans le bled.

Shiba

J'accuse les politiquarts cameriens
D'être non seulement mboutoucous
But en même temps des feymans.
Je les accuse tous—opposants et Rdépécistes
Because ils ne font que pratiquer la belly politics.

J'accuse les tontons macoutes ongolais
Etant donné que dem don ton be na
Les vampires de la République.
Mola, langua-moi!
Comment toi même tu nyè cette aff, no?

Est-ce ma tchat c'est seulement le sissia?
Whether na Paul Biya
Or c'est Ni John Fru Ndi, ou Ndam Njoya,
N'est-ce pas eux tous, ils mangent le même soya?
How you check say dem fit tok true tok?

Vraiment, où est la différence,
Que ce soit Popol ou l'originaire de Ntarikon à Etoudi,
N'est-ce pas dem all na kick pipo?
Na wa for dis we own kondre-o!
Nos politiquarts nous font voir kan-kan wahala.

J 'accuse les politiquarts ongolais
Because ils sont tous les kickmans,
Transformés en élus du peuple.
Je veux qu'on les foute tous en taule
Yes mbombo, dat be say dem must yua ngata!

We don tok! One day one day
Ali Baba et ses quarante voleurs
Must yua ngata, sans oublier le bao locataire
Du quat du peuple à Etoudi
Because Popol sep sep na popo Kengué.

Manioc

Touche pas à mon manioc!
Est-ce une maladie ordinaire
Une wolowoss qui aime une wolowoss?
Qu'est-ce qu'elles se disent au bled?
Make we go nyoxer?
Y-a-t-il un Dieu qui nous protège?

Touche pas à mon manioc!
Est-ce une maladie ordinaire
Une nga qui aime une nga?
Qu'est-ce qu'elles se disent for bed?
Make we go tchouquer?
Y-a-t-il un Dieu qui nous protège?

Touche pas à mon manioc!
Est-ce une maladie ordinaire
Un mola qui aime un mola?
Qu'est-ce qu'ils se disent au long?
Make we go knack kanda?
Y-a-t-il un Dieu qui nous protège?

Touche pas à mon manioc!
Est-ce une maladie ordinaire
Un padre qui aime les mômes?
Qu'est-ce qu'ils se disent à la sacristie?
Make we go knack kanda?
Y-a-t-il un Dieu qui protège les tchotchoros?

Touche pas à mon manioc!
Drôle de temps sur la planète

Y-a-t-il un lieu qui nous protège?
Drôle de moeurs sur la terre
Véritable come no go.
Dis kan manioc na daso allô!

Massa Inoni

Chief Inoni Ephraim
Achouka ngongoli for check say you be frog!
Au fait, me I di askam say hein,
Ce Massa Inoni il était même quoi au palais d'Etoudi?
Planton, nchinda ou chef de terre?

Chief Inoni Ephraim
Aschouka for mimba say
Etoudi na youa own chasse gardée!
Et ton rôle l'affaire Albatros?
Did you have a hand in it ou pas?

Or alors tu n'es qu'un bouc émissaire
Comme les autres malheureux.
Les Camers know ce qui s'est passé
Avec les mbourous de l'ancien chaud gars,
Chef traditionnel du palais d'Etoudi.

Chief Inoni Ephraim
Achouka ngongoli!
Today, te voilà alors en train de crever
Dans les ténèbres de Kondengui
Way no man no sabi pourquoi.

A qui alors la faute? A toi ou à Popol?
Cheh! Le Cameroun c'est le Cameroun!
Mais au lieu de garder son tchinda dans la taule
A perpétuité better Popol dis à Massa Inoni
To back dos et retrouver sa liberté provisoire.

GENEROUS GRACE

2 Corinthians 8:1-15

A central theme in 2 Corinthians is the dynamic difference that God's grace makes in the lives and attitudes of his people. God's grace extends even to that sensitive issue of what we do with our money. So what does grace have to do with our checkbooks? Paul devotes two chapters to the grace of giving.

1. Think of a time when the act of giving was a source of joy and satisfaction to you. What made it so?

Read 2 Corinthians 8:1-15.

2. Paul pointed to other believers and to Jesus as examples of the grace of giving. What do you learn about giving through the example of the Macedonians (verses 1-5)? Find as many principles of giving as you can.

How does Jesus' example motivate you to be generous (verse 9)?

◆ **3.** Explore the contrasts of verse 2. Have you seen or heard about examples of this kind of response in contemporary believers? In what ways have you been challenged to give or to grow by the example of others?

♦ **4.** Look at each use of the word "grace" in the first nine verses. What does grace have to do with giving?

5. The Corinthians had started a collection for the distressed Christians in Jerusalem, but they had not completed it. Why might they have hesitated to act (verse 12)?

♦ **6.** How might the equality principle in verses 13-15 help you decide priorities in giving?

7. If Paul were writing to your church or to your family, what do you think he would say to you about giving?

8. If your checkbook were used to grade your giving, how would you rate?

9. How does this passage challenge you to give beyond your own circle? How might this study group help you to broaden your vision for the world?

GLAD GIVERS

2 Corinthians 8:16–9:15

Fund-raising appeals scream at us from every direction—telethons, letters filled with underlined requests, and high-pressure offering pleas.

Paul's approach to fund raising was quite different. Though he was very direct, he did not need to resort to gimmicks and pressure. Instead, he taught that we cannot outgive a God who lavishes his grace on us. Trusting this generous God releases us from bondage to the material and frees us to give gladly.

1. What positive or negative experiences have you had in connection with fund-raising appeals?

Read 2 Corinthians 8:16–9:5.

◆ **2.** Describe the team Paul is sending to the Corinthians (verses 16-24). What do you learn about Paul and his relationship to other believers in these verses?

3. What are Paul's motives in this fund-raising campaign?

◆ **4.** What potential problems does he face in this collection?

♦ **5.** Paul has been boasting about the Macedonians to the Corinthians (8:1-5) and now he tells of his boasting to the Macedonians about the Corinthians! What does this tell you about Paul?

6. Why does Paul want the Corinthians to be ready with their gift (verses 3-5)?

Read 2 Corinthians 9:6-15.

7. Do you think Paul is teaching so-called "prosperity theology" in this passage (that faith in God will make us wealthy, healthy, and successful)? What do you think it means to "be made rich in every way" (verse 11)?

8. What basic fear does Paul address in verse 8? Note the uses of the word "all" in this verse. What does this convey to you?

♦ **9.** According to this passage, for what purposes does God bless his people?

♦ **10.** What further principles of giving do you learn from this passage?

11. What would it take for you to become a more
generous, cheerful giver (a change in your salary, time
priorities, spending habits, world vision)?

12. Take some time to give thanks for God's great gift
(8:9 and 9:15).

A WOUNDED HEALER

2 Corinthians 10–11

The tone of Paul's letter becomes decidedly more assertive in chapters 10–11 as he defends his position of leadership. His opponents were false teachers (Judaizers) who were trying to undermine his authority. Because this is a letter, we have only one side of the conversation—Paul's reply. We have to try to deduce what the charges were by Paul's answers. Throughout the passage, Paul apologizes because he has to use methods of defense that are completely distasteful to him. He knows that it is not really his honor that is at stake, but the honor of Jesus Christ. He defends himself, not for his own sake, but for the sake of the gospel. We might expect Paul to elaborate on all of his ministry successes. But the résumé Paul presents consists of a list of sufferings. His credentials are his scars.

1. How do you usually react when your motives are misunderstood?

Read 2 Corinthians 10.

2. What is the basis of Paul's appeal to his critics (verse 1)? What might this indicate about the way he hopes to deal with his accusers?

3. What is the first accusation Paul deals with (verses 1 and 10)? What is Paul's response?

♦ **4.** What are the standards and weapons of this world that Paul refers to in verses 2-4?

♦ **5.** What does Paul claim for the weapons he uses? What might these weapons be?

6. What does Paul see as the purpose for the authority God gave him (verse 8)?

7. What standards of measurement are Paul's accusers using (verses 7 and 12)? What are Paul's standards (verses 12-18)?

8. What is one of Paul's primary motives in wanting to clear up the misunderstandings (verses 15-16)? How much does this goal motivate you?

Read 2 Corinthians 11.

◆ **9.** What clues of Paul's fatherly concern for the Corinthians do you see in this chapter?

10. What are Paul's motives in challenging the so-called "super-apostles" (verses 1-13)?

◆ **11.** Why would Paul refuse to be supported by the Corinthians, yet accept help from the Macedonian churches?

◆ **12.** What do you learn about Paul through his "list of boastings"? How does verse 30 summarize Paul's view of success?

13. What can we learn about godly leadership in these two chapters?

THORNS AND GRACE

2 Corinthians 12:1-10

Throughout this very personal book, Paul has opened up his life with complete honesty. Now he peels back yet another layer, exposing what most would consider a crippling liability for ministry. Paul would never have passed the physical exam for modern-day missions organizations! But rather than detracting from his ministry, Paul's weakness became a means of grace for supernatural strength.

1. What do you consider your greatest strength? Your greatest weakness?

Read 2 Corinthians 12:1-10.

♦ **2.** "The third heaven" (verse 2) was a Jewish expression for the immediate presence of God. What few details does Paul reveal about this experience? Why might he speak of himself in the third person?

3. What danger can come from special revelations such as Paul describes? What kept Paul from this danger?

4. The nature of Paul's thorn is uncertain, but it was probably a physical ailment such as malaria, epilepsy, or eye trouble (see Galatians 4:15 and 6:11). The Greek word for "thorn" carries the idea of a sharpened wooden shaft, a stake, or a splinter. What can we know about Paul's thorn from this passage?

5. What was Satan's part in this thorn? What was God's part?

◆ **6.** Contrast the two experiences Paul describes in verses 1-6 and 7-10. How do the two belong together?

◆ **7.** Paul's opponents may have seen his thorn as a punishment from God. How did Paul view it?

8. What can we learn about prayer from Paul's experience?

9. What have you asked God to take away from your life? How has he responded?

10. How has God used weakness in your life to show his strength?

11. What implications for ministry can you glean from Paul's thorn experience?

WARNING AND BLESSING

2 Corinthians 12:11–13:14

Paul considered his authority over the Corinthians as a gift to be used carefully for strengthening the believers. Since his authority was given to him by God (13:10), he could trust God to vindicate him. He wasn't interested in controlling the Corinthians, but in building them up. Instead of manipulating them, Paul wanted them to respond freely to God. His closing warnings and blessings overflow from his fatherlike love for those under his care.

1. What do you remember as your parents' favorite "piece of advice" to you?

Read 2 Corinthians 12:11–13:14.

2. Though he obviously dislikes doing so, how does Paul compare himself with the "super-apostles"?

3. What do you think Paul's tone of voice is in 12:13—exasperated? Sarcastic? Sincere?

4. What fears does Paul express in verses 20-21?

♦ **5.** What can the Corinthians expect from Paul's third visit to them?

♦ **6.** How do Paul's thoughts about weakness and strength in chapter 13 summarize the whole book?

♦ **7.** How would you summarize Paul's "philosophy of ministry"? (Consider the whole book, but especially focus on 12:19 and 13:10.)

8. Instead of criticizing Paul, what should the Corinthians be doing (13:5)? What is Paul's major concern in this challenge he gives them?

9. Who are the people you influence? What have you learned from 2 Corinthians about using that influence effectively?

10. What final commands does Paul give in his closing? Which one do you or your church most need to heed?

◆ **11.** Look carefully at the often-quoted benediction in verse 14. What natural progression of Christian experience do you see expressed here? Pray this benediction as a closing blessing.

LEADER'S NOTES

■ Study 1/Comforted to Comfort

Question 1. Each study will begin with an "approach question" to help group members begin to think about the topic in terms of their own experience. Discuss this question before reading the Scripture passage.

Question 2. Encourage group members to look closely at the greeting in verse 1. Paul writes as an apostle, chosen by the will of God.

Question 6. Some group members may feel encouraged by seeing what Paul was able to endure. Others may feel intimidated by such a man. But Paul is careful to point out that it was only by relying on God that he was able to endure. God, "who raises the dead," will be with us through every peril we face.

Questions 11-12. You may be able to begin applying this Scripture even now in your group. Be sensitive to the responses given and look for ways to encourage group members with the ultimate comfort that comes from God's grace and peace. Be challenged also to look beyond your group to those who need God's comfort.

■ Study 2/Tough Love

Question 2. Paul had already made two visits to Corinth—the first time to found the church there and a second "painful" visit to deal with a difficult discipline problem. He had also written them a severe letter that we no longer have, though some scholars think that chapters 10–13 of 2 Corinthians are part of it. Because of the painful visit and letter, relationships between Paul and the Corinthians were very strained. Paul had planned to visit them again (1:15), but changed his plan to prevent them from further pain. His opponents used this as an opportunity to accuse him of being fickle or unreliable.

Question 4. Perhaps Paul's opponents were saying, "If we can't depend on Paul to do what he said he would do, maybe we can't believe what he told us about God." Paul says that all of God's promises are "Yes" in Christ. William Barclay comments, "He means this—had Jesus never come we might have doubted the tremendous and precious promises of God. We might have argued that they were too good to be true. But a God who loves us so much that He gave us His Son is quite certain to fulfill every promise that He ever made. . . . Jesus is the personal guarantee of God that the greatest and the least of God's promises must all be true" *(Letters to Corinthians, The Daily Study Bible*, p. 196. Edinburgh: Saint Andrew Press, 1973).

Question 5. Since Corinth was the commercial center of the empire, it's interesting to note the trading metaphors Paul uses in 2 Corinthians 1:22: seal of ownership, deposit, and guarantee.

Question 7. It was painful for Paul to rebuke the Corinthians, but tough love demanded that he do it. He rebuked them in love, not to cause pain but to restore joy. Though he rebuked the Corinthians, he did not want to domineer them (2 Corinthians 1:24). Paul speaks openly of joy, distress, anguish, tears, and love—an intimate portrait of a great saint.

Question 8. Ralph Martin explains, "Paul has been slandered, probably to his face, by an unnamed individual. A majority of the Corinthian congregation has agreed to some sort of disciplinary action against him, but only after the seriousness and wider meaning of the offense has been brought home by Paul's tearful letter. Confident now of the church's obedience, he writes again about the matter, this time urging that the offending party be forgiven and brought back into the Christian community" *(2 Corinthians, Word Biblical Commentary*, p. 168. Waco, Tex.: Word, 1986).

Question 9. Paul's motive for discipline was correction, not vengeance. His goal was to build up the offender, not knock him down. He realized that over-severity could drive him from the church and into Satan's hold. He urged discipline that would encourage rather than discourage the offender. He was not advocating "cheap grace," but affirming that genuine repentance should be followed by genuine forgiveness.

■ Study 3/Living Letters

Question 2. In the middle of discussing his trip to Macedonia, Paul breaks off into a discussion of ministry that continues for several chapters. He resumes the story of his trip to Macedonia in 2 Corinthians 7:5.

Question 5. Paul borrows the analogy of a Roman victory procession in verses 14-16. It was customary for the Roman general to display his treasures and captives amidst a cloud of incense. For the victors, this smell was sweet; for the captives, it was the stench of death. Likewise, the gospel is good news to those who believe and repulsive to those who refuse it.

Question 10. 2 Corinthians 3:4-6 expresses a theme that will recur throughout this book—our confidence and competence for ministry must be centered in God.

■ Study 4/Unfading Glory

Question 2. Paul begins his description of the new covenant in verse 6. Encourage group members to look at the whole passage for contrasts between the old and the new covenants.

This passage is not meant to indicate that the law given at Sinai was bad or evil. The problem with the law was that while it exposed sin, it could not take it away. The coming of Christ provided forgiveness for the condemned sinner.

Question 4. Encourage group members to find several practical results such as boldness, understanding, freedom, and a reflection of Christ's glory.

Question 6. The treasure refers back to 2 Corinthians 4:4 where Paul speaks of "the light of the gospel."

Question 7. Paul speaks of "setting forth the truth plainly." He emphasize that Jesus Christ is the theme of the message. There is no room for self-importance or conceit—all the glory belongs to God. 2 Corinthians 4:13 indicates that faith leads to testimony—"I believed; therefore I have spoken."

■ **Study 5/ At Home with the Lord**

Question 2. Tents are temporary and vulnerable structures. Paul uses this image to show the transient nature of our bodies. This passage is another variation on Paul's theme of strength and weakness as he describes the earthly tent and the eternal home.

Question 4. Paul doesn't see eternity as an escape into nothingness, but as entry into a new body where service can be complete.

Question 6. Paul is convinced that even in this life believers can enjoy the foretaste of eternal life. The Christian is a citizen of two worlds, with one foot in time and one in eternity.

Question 10. Paul eagerly anticipates the eternal home, but he reminds us that we must also face judgment. The choices we make in life determine our eternal destiny.

■ **Study 6/Ambassadors for Christ**

Question 1. Take some time to hear from each group member about his or her introduction to the gospel. This can be a powerful introduction to today's passage as well as a time to know one another in new ways.

Question 2. Paul is motivated both by fear of the Lord (2 Corinthians 5:11) and by Christ's love (verse 14). Both are legitimate and necessary reasons for being involved in the ministry of reconciliation.

Question 5. Verse 21 is one of the most powerful statements of God's gift of reconciliation—our sin was exchanged for Christ's righteousness. This allows us to become new creatures (2 Corinthians 5:17).

Question 8. Help group members to see resources such as endurance, hard work, purity, understanding, patience, kindness, love, the Holy Spirit, truthfulness, the power of God, and "weapons of righteousness." Paul summarizes his resources with the familiar theme of strength through weakness—"having nothing, and yet possessing everything."

▌ Study 7/Purity and Promise

Question 2. "The concept of the 'unequal yoke' comes from Deuteronomy 22:10, 'Thou shalt not plow with an ox and an ass together.' The ox was a clean animal to the Jews, but the ass was not . . . and it would be wrong to yoke them together. Furthermore, they have two opposite natures and would not even work well together. It would be cruel to bind them to each other. In the same way, it is wrong for believers to be yoked together with unbelievers" (Warren Wiersbe, *Be Encouraged*, p. 74. Wheaton, Ill.: Victor Books, 1988).

Question 6. In our desire for holy living, we must not isolate ourselves from the people who need our ministry most. Jesus was a "friend of publicans and sinners," yet he was holy and undefiled.

Question 9. Godly sorrow produces true repentance that will be demonstrated in action. Worldly sorrow might characterize someone who is only sorry when caught or someone who is burdened by guilt with no hope for forgiveness.

▌ Study 8/Generous Grace

Question 3. Suffering often helps us to focus attention on others' needs. One study showed that churches in small towns and farming communities gave a higher percentage of their budgets to missions than did metropolitan churches—despite drought, grain embargoes, and tough economic times.

Question 4. Your group may benefit by looking up the word "grace" in a dictionary. The kind of giving described by Paul is not natural; it is supernatural—a result of God's grace.

Question 6. In verse 15, Paul illustrates the equality principle with the miracle of manna in the wilderness (Exodus 16:18). "No matter how much manna the Jews gathered each day, they always had what they needed. Those who tried to hoard the manna discovered that it was impossible, because the manna would decay and smell. The lesson is clear: gather what you need, share what you can, and don't try to hoard God's blessings. God will see to it that you will not be in need if you trust Him and obey His Word" *(Be Encouraged,* p. 89).

■ Study 9/Glad Givers

Question 2. We don't know the identity of the two "brothers" who would accompany Titus. Luke and Barnabas have been suggested as possibilities. Focus on the characteristics Paul mentions about these men. Paul depended on other believers to help him in his ministry. He was a "team player," not a "lone ranger."

Question 4. Paul knew that his critics could accuse him of taking part of this collection for his own use. So he took steps to ensure that others would share with him the task of taking the collection to Jerusalem.

Question 5. This is a delightful look at Paul's humanity and greatness. After praising the Corinthians to the Macedonians, he's a bit afraid that the Corinthians might let him down. But the passage also shows Paul's great heart—praising one church to another rather than pointing out their failings.

Questions 9-10. Be sure that your group uses all of 2 Corinthians 9:6-15 in answering these two questions.

■ Study 10/A Wounded Healer

Question 4. The standards and weapons of this world are based on human ideas of power and strength—getting ahead, polishing speaking skills, "dressing for success," and establishing superiority.

Question 5. Paul looks to Jesus' example of meekness and gentleness, realizing that meekness is not weakness. His weapons may have included prayer, the Word of God, love, and the power of the Spirit.

Question 9. Paul uses the picture of a loving father who has a daughter engaged to be married. He is jealous for that daughter's purity and wants to protect her so she can be kept pure. In 2 Corinthians 11:7-12, Paul speaks of the sacrifice he has made to provide for the Corinthians—another fatherly privilege and duty. In verse 28, he describes his concern for the Corinthians. Every father (and godly leader) understands the kind of anxiety Paul describes.

Question 11. Paul did not want the preaching of the gospel to be hindered in any way. He did not want to take support unless it was freely offered. (The "super-apostles" may have been demanding support—2 Corinthians 11:20.) Receiving support from one community to minister to another is a commendable approach, though an established congregation has a duty to support its workers.

Question 12. Some of Paul's sufferings for Christ are described in the book of Acts, though there are many for which we have no record besides this brief list. Christianity was no "crutch" for Paul! If he had not been an apostle, he would not have suffered these trials, but he did so gladly for the praise of God (2 Corinthians 11:31).

■ Study 11/Thorns and Grace

Question 2. God gave Paul various visions and revelations (Acts 9:3; 16:9; 22:17), but we do not have a specific record of this particular revelation elsewhere in Scripture. Jewish rabbis spoke about themselves in the third person, and Paul adopted that approach here, possibly because it would sound less boastful.

Question 6. "Paul went from paradise to pain, from glory to suffering. He tasted the blessing of God in heaven and then felt the buffeting of Satan on earth. He went from ecstasy to agony, and yet the two experiences belong together. His one experience of glory prepared him for the constant experience of suffering, for he knew that God was able to meet his need. Paul had gone to heaven—but then he learned that heaven could come to him" (Warren Wiersbe, *Be Encouraged,* p. 138).

Question 7. While Paul's opponents may have seen his thorn as a punishment, Paul was able to see it as a gift from God. Paul's burden carried him to God. His thorn became an asset rather than a liability because of God's grace. (The Greek tense in 2 Corinthians 12:9 indicates continuous action—God's grace is continually sufficient for whatever comes up in life.)

■ Study 12/Warning and Blessing

Question 5. Paul has already visited the Corinthians twice—first to found the church, and second to deal with their disciplinary problems. The second visit was the "painful visit," which Paul hopes not to repeat on his third visit. But he is ready to confront the wrongdoers who are not yet repentant (2 Corinthians 12:21) and to discipline them if necessary.

Question 6. The Corinthians and Paul viewed power very different-ly. They were looking for forceful personalities and spectacular actions. Paul had learned the power of strength through weakness—human weakness as a vehicle for supernatural power.

Question 7. Paul was clearly the leader of the Corinthians and didn't apologize for his authority. But he recognized his authority as a gift, and he used it for strengthening and building up the believers. He never lost sight of his ultimate purpose—"praise be to the God and Father of our Lord Jesus Christ" (2 Corinthians 1:3). Paul lived by faith, not by sight (5:7) and he saw his ministry as a gift of God's mercy (4:1). Though the Corinthians were stubborn and rebellious, Paul saw great potential in them because of God's grace and recon-ciliation (5:17). He didn't regard anyone "from a worldly point of view," and so he expressed great confidence in the Corinthians (7:4). At the same time, he challenged and rebuked them, longing to see them "abound in every good work" (9:8).

Question 11. Note the reference to the Trinity in the benediction. The terms grace, love, and fellowship depict progression from salvation to continuing growth and outreach in a believer's life. All of us desperately need these blessings of grace, love, and com-munion in our lives today as God strengthens us to serve a needy world.

WHAT SHOULD WE STUDY NEXT?

To help your group answer that question, we've listed the Fisherman Guides by category so you can choose your next study.

TOPICAL STUDIES

Becoming Women of Purpose, Barton

Building Your House on the Lord, Brestin

Discipleship, Reapsome

Doing Justice, Showing Mercy, Wright

Encouraging Others, Johnson

Examining the Claims of Jesus, Brestin

Friendship, Brestin

The Fruit of the Spirit, Briscoe

Great Doctrines of the Bible, Board

Great Passages of the Bible, Plueddemann

Great People of the Bible, Plueddemann

Great Prayers of the Bible, Plueddemann

Growing Through Life's Challenges, Reapsome

Guidance & God's Will, Stark

Higher Ground, Brestin

How Should a Christian Live? (1,2, & 3 John), Brestin

Marriage, Stevens

Moneywise, Larsen

One Body, One Spirit, Larsen

The Parables of Jesus, Hunt

Prayer, Jones

The Prophets, Wright

Proverbs & Parables, Brestin

Relationships, Hunt

Satisfying Work, Stevens & Schoberg

Senior Saints, Reapsome

Sermon on the Mount, Hunt

The Ten Commandments, Briscoe

When Servants Suffer, Rhodes

Who Is Jesus? Van Reken

Worship, Sibley

BIBLE BOOK STUDIES

Genesis, Fromer & Keyes

Job, Klug

Psalms, Klug

Proverbs: Wisdom That Works, Wright

Ecclesiastes, Brestin

Jonah, Habakkuk, & Malachi, Fromer & Keyes

Matthew, Sibley

Mark, Christensen

Luke, Keyes

John: Living Word, Kuniholm

Acts 1-12, Christensen

Paul (Acts 13-28), Christensen

Romans: The Christian Story, Reapsome

1 Corinthians, Hummel

Strengthened to Serve (2 Corinthians), Plueddemann

Galatians, Titus & Philemon, Kuniholm

Ephesians, Baylis

Philippians, Klug

Colossians, Shaw

Letters to the Thessalonians, Fromer & Keyes

Letters to Timothy, Fromer & Keyes

Hebrews, Hunt

James, Christensen

1 & 2 Peter, Jude, Brestin

How Should a Christian Live? (1, 2 & 3 John), Brestin

Revelation, Hunt

BIBLE CHARACTER STUDIES

Ruth & Daniel, Stokes

David: Man after God's Own Heart, Castleman

Job, Klug

King David: Trusting God for a Lifetime, Castleman

Elijah, Castleman

Men Like Us, Heidebrecht & Scheuermann

Peter, Castleman

Paul (Acts 13-28), Christensen

Great People of the Bible, Plueddemann

Women Like Us, Barton

Women Who Achieved for God, Christensen

Women Who Believed God, Christensen

Si Chief Inani dit non
Son mandat va bolè à Kondengui
Car qui vole un oeuf, vole un boeuf.
Famille-o! Famille! Comment vous-mêmes
Vous nyè ce tchat no?

Ashawo Man Pikin

DSK, c'est un vrai ashawo!
Soso nioxer, dasso tchouquer!
Chouchou des nanas de toutes les couleurs
No bi na shame dis for nation française?
Homme incarcéré par sa propre libido.

DSK, c'est un vrai wolowoss!
Nyoxer à droit, nyoxer à gauche!
Bête noire de la communauté des femelles
Bipède aux prises avec son propre bangala!
Victime de sa propre volupté sexuelle.

DSK, c'est un véritable akwara!
Proxénète, Pute, Nymphomane.
Horreur des ngas mariées,
«Argent en main, caleçon en bas »
Putain ! Pagaille ! Pitié !

Al-Qaeda

Al-Qaeda,
Come no go for upside.
Epithète qui fait trémousser
Homme, femme et gosse!
Al-Qaeda, na ndoutou, dit-on.

Al-Qaeda,
Au fait, wusai dem commot?
Qui sont-ils ? D'où viennent-ils ?
Ja wanda seulement.
Secte, religion, confrérie ou bande de terroristes?

Certes, devrions-nous poser
Cette question épineuse à l'épine dorsale
De la mouvance—Osama Bin Laden.
Dommage qu'il soit crevé.
Confrérie aux mobiles louches implantée partout.

Grand Camarade

Grand Camarade, El Hajj
Je check say nous tous on le know.
Ce dictateur qui avait foutu le Cameroun
En l'air avant de donner
Son chia à son nchinda—ancien chaud gars.
Ce bandit beti qui plume le Cameroun à vue d'oeil.

Il est bien vrai que les politiquarts
Sont one and the same partout sur notre planète.
C'est même pour cela que je wanda
Au sujet des dépouilles du Grand Camarade,
Abandonnées à Dakar depuis from.
Why must Ahijdo's remains stay in Dakar?

Je wanda surtout why Popol
N'a pas utilisé son number six pour
Fait venir la carcasse de ce pauvre
Musulman whey yi been dash yi chia.
Pourquoi ne pas ramener ses dépouilles
Ne serait-ce que pour calmer les esprits troublés?

Il y a des taras qui nous remplissent
Les oreilles avec leur ntamulung choir
Selon lequel Grand Camarade fut
Un meilleur kamambrou que Popol
Je leur tok carrément de shut up,
Parce qu'ils ne savent rien de ce qu'ils langua.

Ces mbombos n'ont qu'à aller tchatcher avec
Les baos comme Reuben Um Nyobé,

Ernest Ouandié, Félix Moumié, Albert Ndongmo,
Albert Womah Mukong et Wambo le Courant,
And then dem go sabi pourquoi je check say
Grand Camarade était un diable comme les autres.

Au vu de ces choses
Faudrait-il peut-être langua que
Un bon politiquart na daso
De one way yi don meng,
Autrement dit, il faut être cadavéré
Pour être un bon politiquart.

Mola, how you sep you nyè dis palava no?
Les camers plenty ont tchatté à Mbiya que,
Non, non et non, vous ne pouvez pas
Abandonner l'ancien kamambrou
Dans une piètre sépulture dans un quat étranger.
Soyons sérieux! 6 avril ou non.

Même so, Popo reste impertubable
Hanté comme il est
By the ghost of Grand Camarade.
Il ne veut carrément ya nothing
A propos de cette affaire vachement politisée.
Les appels sont tombés sur les deaf ears!

Dommage au Grand Camarade
Qui n'a jamais pris le temps de bien connaître
Le mec Beti à qui il avait largué son chia,
Ce scélérat connu sous le nom de Paul Biya.
Je dirais donc au Grand Camarade, Achouka !

Pont De Wouri

One sharp sharp matin
For cinq heures for Pont de Wouri,
Them langua we say:
Il y a la guerre à Douala!
Them say war done commot for Pont de Wouri-o!

One sharp sharp morning
Pont de Wouri na champ de bataille
Il y a la guerre; il y a ceci cela!
Tremblement de terre
Par ci, par là!

Nous wandarons que mais qu'est-ce qu'il y a?
Kamambrou for Douala yi say,
Il y a la guerre; il y a ceci cela!
Yi send ba gendarmes, ba mange-mille.
Et tout; et tout, Par ci, par là!

Ba militaires dem,
Them tanap side by side
Ba di wan for ndiba
Ba di wan for up
Them tanap prêts à tirer sur qui que ce soit.

Sep so, one small kamabrou
Il est passé par où?
Selling after the market?
Popo me I di askam say hein,
Qui avait organisé ce movie?

Au fait qui était derrière ce coma
De double zéro sept?
For Pont de Wouri
One sharp sharp cinq heures for Douala
Question de temps; on va know biensûr!

Chairman

Quand on est vieux,
On est vieux no be so?
Le pouvoir appartient
A ceux qui se lèvent tôt.
Laissez-moi tchatcher la vérité à Fru Ndi.

If you want say make some man
Gee chance for road, you sep must
Learn for gee chance for road
For some other mola
Wey yi dey for youa back.

The truth of the matter be say,
Charity begins at home.
We be di check say sometime
Chairman go gee chance for some jeune talent
Make yi corriger Pa Pol.

But sep so, Pa for Ntarikon say
Ngumba must cry for Etoudi,
Yi say Ngumba close must enter Palais.
Ah ah, Je wanda que depuis 1990
This vieux capable don be katika
For SDF jusqu'ai ce jour!

Time waits for nobody
If we want make some man for gee
Chance for road, we sep must
Learn for gee chance for ala man
Way yi day for we back.

Français Mboko

Camfranglais, Français makro
Le tchat du quat,
Langua des débrouillards—
Sauveteurs, bendskineurs, pousseurs,
Taximans, wolowoss, chargeurs,
Bayam sellams, call-boxeurs, feymans.

Où est la différence?
Il s'agit du parler du terroir:
Je parle camerounais,
Donc je suis Camer.
Tchatchons le Camfranglais seulement.
N'en déplaise aux saras.

Ayez l'avant-goût de notre tchat du terroir:
Attisé ainsi, tu serais ridicule,
Et moi j'aurais raison de
Montrer mes attrape-maniocs,
Autrement dit, je me moquerais gentiment de toi.
Comme tu nyè, le langua des camers est bien chouette.

Mami Wata

Chantal Pulchérie Vigouroux Biya,
La belle de la République
Ou mami wata qui bouffe
Les mbourous de notre cher pays?

This nkane elle est même quoi?
La mami wata de la République
Ou bien notre première dame?
Je wanda seulement-o
Because si vraiment elle est notre first lady

Pourquoi alors elle sape
Comme une vraie wolowoss?
Est-ce seulement pour attirer
Les yos et les jeunes talents
Etant donné que son ancien chaud gars

Is no longer très chaud?
Ekié! Je wanda only.
Ou alors c'est pour show off tout court
Comme c'est le petit modèle des metoches?
Nous voulons sabi quand même.

Chantal Pulchérie Vigouroux Biya,
Avec le nkap du peuple camerounais
Qu'elle a kick de la caisse noire d'Etoudi,
Elle est devenue mami wata, mini minor
On top of being notre première dame!

C'est Popol qui a cherché
And he don trouva
Just now he must supporta
And for dat supporta
Il faut se méfier car la femme qui a connu la rue…

Bagdad

Ngola na Bagdad?
Quelle guerre politique!
Tu go à Mamfe, il y a la guerre
Entre Agbor Tabi et Paul Ayah.
Them day à couteaux tirés.

Ngola no be Bagdad.
Quelle guerre politique!
Tu go à Tiko, il y a le feu d'artifice.
Affaire ngrafis contre sons of the soil.
L'un veut tuer l'autre.

Ngola no be Nagasaki and Hiroshima.
You go for Nkambe,
Il y a la guerre politique.
Na Awudu Mbaya Ibrahim
And Yembe Shey Jones qui s'entretuent.

Bamenda no be Vietnam.
Tu go à Abakwa,
Il y a la guerre politique.
Atanga and Angwafor veulent chasser Fru Ndi,
Them say Chairman doit rentrer à Baba.

Ngoketunjia don ton be na Waterloo
Tu go à Ndop,
Il y a la guerre politique.
Docta Lesigha and Fon Doh
Them no want see eye to eye.

Quand alors la fin de ce brouhaha?
Les élus du peuple sont-ils cinglés
Or alors them don crish daso?
Je wanda seulement, hein.
How you sep nyè dis affaire no mbomo?

Ndamba

Koukouma, you must sabi
Say dis youa own équipe Lions Domptables
Que vous avez formée c'est seulement le sissia.
Vous avez trop échoué,
Défaite sur défaite, comment!

Kamambrou,
Il faut know que ndamba na sense
Ndamba ce n'est pas le boum boum!
If your joueurs them di mouiller
It's your faut car c'est vous le coach.

Koukouma,
Pour marquer les buts
Il faut éviter le boum boum!
Mola, ndamba na sense
Ndamba no be tchouquer tchouquer.

Coach, vous avez trop échoué,
You must give chance
For ala man better than you are
Ancien chaud gars,
Your mandat don bolè.

Youa Lions Domptables
Na distributeurs de points
Vos joueurs sont les loss-sense.
You must démissioner! Step down!
Like your répé way been dash you chia!

Démissionnez! Step down!
Parce que vos joueurs
Ne font que ndima ndima
Ils ne font que njoum njoum! Step down!
Si non le peuple vous demandera leur compte!

Bakassi

Bakassi na no man's land.
Sometime me I di wanda say hein,
Who owns the land à Bakassi?
Finalement, si Popol check say il a eu gain de cause
Je lui dirai tout simplement que c'est lui le vrai mougou.

Vous savez que les Biafrais
Ne lâchent pas facilement
So no, même si la CPI a tranché l'affaire Bakassi,
Faudrait toujours rester à la qui-vive.
Parce que with les Biafrais you never know!

Avec ces mboms aussi têtus que les cochons
You only have to sleep avec un seul oeil fermé.
Donc, je dirais au Kamambrou,
Chef de terre de Bakassi,
De faire gaffe!

SONARA

Donc, finalement this SONARA
Don ton be na chasse gardée
Pour les Bassa tout court, hein?
Comment se fait-il que year by year
Il n'y a que les Bassa qui gèrent
Cette richesse pétrolière nationale?

En effet, gérer c'est trop dire,
Faudrait peut-être poser la question autrement
Why is it that seulement the Bassa are deemed
Intelligent enough to mismanage the affairs
Of la Société nationale de raffinage à Limbe, la SONARA?
Nous avons the right to know!

Suite au décès de Bernard Eding (bon débarras!)
Cameroonians heaved a sigh of relief pensant que Popol
Allait choisir quelqu'un with a grain of probity
Pour gérer les affaires de la SONARA. Hélas, manqué de
veine!
Fidèle à ses principes, il a opté pour un fiéfé bandit
Comme lui-même—Charles Metouck comme Katika de la
SONARA

Avec l'arrestation de ce mbom,
Je ya que c'est un certain Ibrahim Talba Malla
Qui devient le Director General of SONARA.
Mais fait quoi fait quoi les Camers finiront par sabi
The truth about toutes les manigances
Qui ont eu lieu à la SONARA depuis Methusalem.

Affaire Anglo

Je ne sais plus qui je suis.
D'autres m'appellent Frog.
Je ne sais pas qui je suis.
Mon nom c'est le Bamenda
Y en a qui m'appellent ennemi dans la maison.
Certains me qualifient de Biafrais et je wanda pourquoi.
Mon nom c'est le citoyen de second degré.
D'autres osent même me donner
L'épithète d'enfant terrible de la famille.

Taisez-vous!
Ne m'embêtez pas!
You don't know que je suis ici au pays natal?
Vous ignorez que mon cordon ombilical est planté ici.
Ecoutez, je me battrai jusqu'à la dernière
Goutte de mon sang
Afin de me forger un vrai nom.
Vous ne m'appellerez plus Anglofrog!
Vous ne m'appellerez jamais Franglo!

Fermez la gueule! Ne me dérangez plus!
Vous ignorez que je suis fils du terroir ?
Vous feignez ne pas savoir que je suis ici au bercail ?
Je me battrai jusqu'au dernier souffle
Pour me façonner une véritable langua qui me sied bien!
Je ne parlerai plus français,
Je parlerai plus English,
C'est-à-dire que désormais, je parlerai Camerounais
Parce qu'ici nous sommes chez nous; à bon entendeur salut!

Ngataman (Hommage A Lapiro)

You fall for ngombe
You make like say you get ntong.
You give me that coup de tête way
You be take sissia Eric Chinje because
You be get ma macabo since year by year.

And how I dong go bata moua
You nyè for that affaire for constitution constipée,
You dong profité for émeutes 2008
You send tapi for my side,
I go boulot njoh ngata for three year…

Donc you must sabi sei popo you
You dong chercha and you dong trouva
And you must supporta!
For da supporta, you must tie heart
You chop maîtrise because say,

Comformément à l'article 19 for
Charte internationale des droits de l'homme,
And according to the motion de soutien
And appel du peuple way my complice them
Dong give me, I go spit fire just now like dragon, Kwaah!

Na tsunami I di déclencher for this heure
I no give kong l'heure!
Popo me I sabi say this tour no be na ngata again,
Na for deme me en direct and I day prêt for meng.
De toutes les façons, I be dong prêté serment
from year by year say I ndomo; donc à luta continua!

Homme-Lion

Ancien chaud gars na mouilleur!
Step down! Démissionnez!
Because you dong over massacré constitution...
You dong over échouer
Subordination du pouvoir judiciaire na you!

Subordination du pouvoir législatif na you!
Manoeuvre politique avec impunité na soso you!
Step down! Démissionnez!
Because you dong over mouiller!
Insécurité généralisée—

Chavoum dong hala for banque for Bonaberi
Fusils dong hala for Pont de Wouri
Dem dong meng your chef de terre,
Kamambrou for Bakassi
You dong over mouiller!

Step down! Démissionnez!
Ngemeng and chômage
Dong multiplié for dis mboko
Bendskinneurs, chauffeurs clandos,
Laveurs de voitures, tackleurs, sauveteurs

Bayam sellams, coiffeurs and coiffeuses ambulantes
For Marché Central, call-boxeurs...
Dem di pointer na for dong rain and for dong sun...
Preuve, dem di kick muna bébés
For maternité everywhere for we own kondre.

No be your boulot na sécurisation
Des personnes et de leurs biens?
A vrai dire this one na échec total
If you no fit garantir sécurité sep for nourrissons!
Step down! Démissionnez! You dong over mouiller!

Méga-Tombe D'après Valsero

Le Cameroun est devenu
Une méga-tombe pour les yos et yoyettes
Ce bled tue les jeunes talents!
Cette génération ne verra pas
Le fameux bout du tunnel
De toutes les façons je n'y crois pas,
La jeunesse crève à petit feu,
Tandis que les vieux derrière leurs châteaux
Se saoulent à l'eau d'odontol,
Ce pays tue les tchotchoros,
Cinquante ans de pouvoir,
Après ça, ils ne lâchent pas le pouvoir
La vie est trop dure au quat.
L'homme-lion la rend encore plus dure,
Il le sait.

A Yaoundé, ils le savent,
Ce pays tue les yos et yoyettes,
Ce pays est comme une bombe à retardement
Pour les jeunes aux tombeaux.
L'homme-lion,
Faites attention,
Quand ça va péter ça va tuer
Tous les lambeaux,
Alors les repés et remés, faites de la place,
Il faut pas le flambeau,
Ce pays tue les munas,
Les vieux ne lâchent pas la prise

Puis-je savoir pourquoi ça ne marche pas au bled
J'ai fait de longues années d'études
Et j'ai pas trouvé le wok
Because ce sont les mêmes qui tiennent la chandelle
Ali Baba et ses quarante kickmans
Vivent au mboa comme s'ils sont de passage
Ils amassent des fortunes, spécialistes de gombo
Ils font preuve d'arrogance, ils frustrent le peuple
Ils piétinent les règles et ils font ce qu'ils veulent.

Le peuple n'en peut plus, les jeunes en ont marre
On veut aussi goûter du miel sinon on te gare
Les jeunes talents ne rêvent plus
Les tchotchoros n'en peuvent plus
La majorité crève
Dans le vice ils basculent
Quand le monde avance, nous,
Au bled, on recule
Le peuple est souverain il n'a jamais tort,
Il a la force du nombre, il peut te donner tort
On n'a pas peur de la meng,
Ils disent de toi que c'est toi "l'homme lion"
Mais ils n'ont qu'un rêve:
Ils veulent tuer le lion!

Zangalewa

A chacun son fusil
A chacun son casque
A chacune ses bottes
A chacune son képi
A vos armes!
Because Ongola est devenu
Un champ de bataille tout court!

J'ai le tong que mon perika est zangalewa.
Quand il touche ses kolos,je peux njoter,
Il me donne des mbourouos pour le jobajo.
Et moi, je poum chez ma ngui,
Toute la nuit on jong des bouteilles de jobajo.
Nous nioxons à mort.
Quand il s'en va à la guerre, moi, je fais des priers,

Je fais des patères austères.
Because c'est une mauvaise guerre,
Une guerre nonsense,
Une guerre incendiaire,
Une guerre meurtrière,
Une guerre suicidaire,
Une guerre insensée comme celle de Bakassi.

Gombistes

Dans la bouche des gombistes
Il n'y a que ce langua:
Mon refré est en haut,
Ma vie va changer,
Vraiment changer!

Le décret vient de tomber
Mon bro vient d'être
Nommé à un poste très élevé.
La rumeur a circulé à la radio trottoir
Aujourd'hui, c'est confirmé.

La radio en a parlé, parlé, parlé.
La télé a confirmé.
ça y est, ma vie va changer,
Vraiment changer!
Never and never ya bad again!

Je vais enfin respirer
Je vais devoir me comporter
Comme un vrai katika
Since mon refré est en haut,
Suffer don finish-o!
Terminé le Johnny,
Terminés les pains chargés,
Les taxis surchargés,
Ma vie va changer,
Vraiment changer!

Je serais véhiculé dans une merco.
J'irai partout dans les quats
Me ballader dans ma merco climatisée,
Toutes les titis vont tomber sans glisser
Je vais gagner des marchés.

My brother est en haut,
Même si je ne peux pas livrer,
Il va quand même me filer du gombo.
Ma vie va changer,
Vraiment changer!

Au village on va fêter,
Au quat on va bouger
On va boire
On va manger
On va sèkèlè.

Palais D'Etoudi

Chez Oncle Sam

Parfois je wanda que
Qu'est-ce qui arrive à ces connards
Qui travaillent ou font semblant de travailler
Au palais du peuple à Washington, D.C.
Tu les appelles à mort,
Il y a nobody pour répondre à ton call, hein !

A ton appel, heh!
Tu vas même là-bas in person,
Ils te parlent comme s'ils viennent
De vider des bouteilles de matango
Ou pire encore d'odontol.
This one is really ndoutou!

Des fois je wanda que
Qu'est-ce qui a même amené ces
Villaconcons chez les nassaras
Où tout le monde se comporte bien
Juste pour qu'ils viennent montrer
Aux saras comment nous les Camers

On est expert en lavage du linge sale en publique.
Vrraiimment!
Même les cauchemars ont des limites!
Sans vous mentir, j'avoue que J'en ai ras le bol
Avec ces fils de chiens qui ne know
Pas comment se comporter au Palais d'Etoudi à D.C.

Docta

Quand je think about les doctas kamerunais
Je wanda que vraiment qu'est-ce qui
Ne va pas avec nos intellos?
Sont-ils tout simplement mboutoucous
Or bien ils ont carrément perdu la boussole?

Prenons le cas de ce fameux
Jacques Famé Ndongo qui se comporte
Comme un Johnny four-foot.
When he says silly things like:
Nous sommes tous les créatures de Paul Biya.

Que veut-il vraiment langua?
Does he mean that tous les Camers
Sont aussi mbout que Popol
Ou bien il veut tok que quoi?
Que les Camers sont tous membres
De la bande d'Ali Baba et les 40 mazembes?

Cheh, je vous dis que
Les intellos kamerunais
Vont nous faire voir de toutes les couleurs
Je dis bien de toutes les couleurs, hein!
C'est vrai que l'impossible n'est pas camerounais
Mais faut pas que les doctas abusent quand même!

Ici au mboa il y a les doctas kan kan:
Tu vas à Ngoa Ekelle,
Tu vas nyè les doctas qui fok
Les yoyettes sur le plancher dans leurs bureaux.

Printed in the United States
by Baker & Taylor Publisher Services

Ahan, n'oubliez pas le langua de deuxième bureau-o.

Tu vas à l'hôpital,
Tu verras les doctas qui nyoxent avec les malades
Croyez-moi mbombo! Pas de toli!
Ce que l'oeil nyè
La bouche ne peut pas refuser de langua.
Doctas dey for Ngola kind by kind.

A Tout Casser Camtok

Massa,
Man don tonton tire
Dis à tout casser tok for dis kontri-o!
You wan pass for any side,
Na daso 'moi parler toi parler',
You wan wake up for sharp sharp,
Na soso 'toi parler moi parler',
You wan nang for last heure,
Na daso à tout casser.
Just now, I dong loss my sense.

For Ngola,
We get tok for Bafut,
We get tok for Bamunka,
We get tok for Banso,
We get tok for Bali,
We get tok for Bambalang,
We get tok for Bamessing,
We get tok for Baba
We get tok for Bafanji,
We get tok for Bamali,
We get tok for Babessi
We get tok for Balimkumbat
We get tok for Bakundu,
We get tok for Bangwa,
We get tok for Bakweri.
We get tok sote pass two Hundred!

Wheti mek we no fit land
We own pikin dem all dis tok dem for sukulu?

Na shame di do we or na daso foolish?
You want pass for any corner,
Na soso 'I was'
You want situp for any side,
Na daso 'Moi parler toi parler'
We'eh! We'eh!
Wheti be we own self wit dis bastard tok dem?

Taim wey you go for village
for do kontri fashion
you go tok na 'I was'?
Taim wey you go for kontri for cry die,
you go cry die na wit 'moi parler toi parler'?

Taim wey you go for village
For knack door for marred some nga
Wey you want marred'am
You go knack door na for French?

Mek wuna no begin fool wuna sef!
White man tok na daso bastard tok.
You no fit lef youa own tok
Go take some ala man yi tok
begin mek nyanga wit'am!

Kontri tok na we own culture.
Kontri tok na we own tradition.
Kontri tok na we own identity
Kontri tok na we own life
Make wuna no make erreur!
Nansara tok na daso allo tok.

Deuxieme Bureau

Some day some man be dei
for long wit yi Nyango.
Dem di dammer.
Dem wan ya telephone hala:
Griiing! Griiing! Griiing!
Nyango jump for table yi go pick phone
Yi amsa sei:'Hallo who is on the line?'

Na yi wei some titi amsa sei: na me Matalina!
Ah! Ah! Dis palava dong pass Nyango.
Yi daso tie hart yi ax'am sei:
you wan tok na for who?
Titi sei: I wan tok na for youa massa.

Eh! Eh! Na which kain ting dis?
Lef small mek Nyango get 'fainting sick'.
Yi soso tie hart, yi axe Matalina sei:
"What business do you have with my husband?"
Just now, yi dong ton na palava for Gramma!

Matalina sei:"The business I have
with your husband is that I'm
his deuxième bureau!"
Dis à tout casser tok yi pass Nyango.
Yi tok for Matalina sei:"Hold on!"
Nyango be cover phone wit yi hand,
Yi put mop for yi massa yi ear yi tok sei:
Na youa disame buro wan tok for you.

Taim we massa dong ya dis tori,
yi be sabi one taim sei na yi njumba
dei for phone.
Yi lef daso small mek yi too katch 'fainting sick'.
Yi begin shek like sei na fever dong katch yi.
Shweat begin commot for yi skin.

Nyango dong nye di palava sotai yi pass yi,
yi ton back for phone yi knack some gramma for Matalina sei:
" My husband is not available now!"
Juaaa! Yi dong knack phone for grong.

How wei Matalina be dong wait sotai
Yi skin begin hot, yi be tok wit vex for Njango sei:
"Tell him that his girlfriend called!"
Eh Maleh! Oh Maleh!
Matter approve himself!
From da day Nyango sabi sei:dis deuxième bureau"palava
Na daso njumba palava.
One taim he start pack yi kaku for commot marred.

So for las heure,
All Mola dem,
All massa dem,
All Mbo'oko dem,
All san-san boy dem,
All nkwankanda dem,
All ashawo manpikin dem,
All akwara husband dem,
Mek wuna sabi sei dis secret
for deuxième bureau no be secret any more!
So no,

All nyango dem,
All titi dem,
All njumba dem,
All small ting dem,
All missus dem,
All marred woman dem,
Me, I di langua wuna sei,
Mek wuna no mek erreur,
bekoz erreur for mbutuku,
na dammer for ndoss!

Taim wey massa sei,
I di go for ma deuxième bureau,
mek wuna no check sei yi di go na for wok,
Wusai! Na kanda yi di go knack'am!
Some titi dei some secteur di wait massa.
Mek wuna put dis tori fain fain for wuna tête!
Na so dis tori for deuxième bureau dei.

A Malin Malin Et Demi

Tif man na come no go.
Na some ma complice
Be tok yi ting sei:
Tif man die, tif man bury'am.
Some panapu no pass dis wan.

For Ongola,
Tif fullup for all side,
All man na tif man:
Patron tif,
Planton tif,
Boss tif,
Messenger tif
Na so gomna of de tif
For de tif
And by de tif dei.
Na so the gospel according
to Biyaism dei.

Commissaire de poice tif,
Sans galons tif,
Superintendent of police tif,
Police constable tif,
Capitaine tif,
Foot soldier tif.

Dem sei if youa broda
Dei for top stick yi di tif,
You must kop nye forseka motoh no moh.
Dem sei if Grand Katika tif,

43

You must kop nye forseka sei,
Le *coup de tête* du Grand Katika
Fit mof youa own garri for mop.
Na so de law according to Mbivodoism dei.

For Ambasonia,
Tif done pass mark-oh!
Woman pikin tif,
Man pikin tif,
Repé tif,
Remé tif
Grand frère tif,
Petit frère tif,
Tchotchoro tif,
Vieux capable tif,
Na so tchop-broke potism dei

For Nooremac
Tif na helele-oh!
Na some ma tara be tok sei jam pass die.
Dem tif nchou for bank,
Dem tif melecin for hospita,
Dem tif moni for school fees,
Dem tif tax moni,
Dem tif stick for Yabassi black bush,
Dem tif oya for Sonara,
Just now dem wan tif sef Bakassi!
Na waa for Mbiya Mbivodo-oh!

Tif man na Manawa-oh!
Tif man di lie sote pass tif dog.
Tif man fit toom sef yi own mami.

44

Tif man di tok daso wit wata for inside yi mop,
Tif man sitdown for youa long,
Na so yi eye go di pass pass
Like sei yi hia na bad news.
Yi di daso check de ting
Wey yi go kick before yi commot.
Tif man na come no go,
Na sick man number one!

Na yi mek tif pipo dem
Get kain by kain name:
Tchong,
Bandit,
Voleur,
Coupeur de route,
Barawo,
Leuh,
Thief,
Robber
Feyman,
Kick man.

Mini-Mignonne

New year, new fashion!
Some wan dong commot just now.
Dem di call'am sei change waka.
You want nye any ngondere,
Yi di daso waka like ntumbu.
All nga dem for Ngola dem di waka
Like sei dem di saka
na ndombolo all di taim!
Dis kain waka dong pass me.

New generation, new fashion!
Some new wan dong commot right now.
Dem di call'am sei mini minor.
You wan nye titi for any corner,
Yi di daso sap na "see ma dross"
Ah,ah! dis palava dong big pass ma head.
Some ma tara for Sasse be call da kain
Cloz sei 'see through'.
Mini mignonne dem na helele-o!

Mini mignonne dem no di gring
Say mek mboti tanap for dem skin.
Soso wear 'see ma bra'
Na so mini minor dem dei!
Soso wear 'see my bombi'

Autres temps, autres moeurs,
Da mean sei: any taim get yi own fashion.
Na so some ma complice
For University of Duala be tok sei:

Na so nouvelle génération dei.

Just now for Nansarwa kontri,
All man pikin dong ton be na mini mignon!
You wan pass for any side,
You di daso nye man pikin wey
Yi trosa di hang na for yi shit hole,
Ah! Ah! Na wheti dipass?
Ah di wanda!

Na some ma tara for Chicago Ghetto
Be tell me sei,
"Man you ain't know what this is all about?
I tell yi sei:
Man, I ain't got no clue.
Yi sei:
It's called saggin' pants!"

Dis saggin' pants
Na pantalon wey yi di daso
Shweep road for Uncle Sam!
Na yi I di wanda sei dis
saggin' pants na wheti?
Na yi da ma tara di tell me
dis tori for saggin'pants.
Da tori shweet sotai tif
man laugh for banda!

Yi sei dis ting be begin'am
Na taim wey Mbere Khaki for America
Dem be tcha black pipo
Go put dem for ngata,

How wey mbere be di fia sei
Ngata pipo dem fit take dem kanda,
Da ting wey mukala dem di call'am sei "belt",
Go hang dem sef, dem be take
all man yi kanda go hide'am.

Ah! Ah! Na yi some sense come enter
For ngata pipo dem head sei,
After all, dem fit try for waka
Wey kanda na dei.
Na yi dem begin waka like
Man pikin wey dem just cut yi bangala.
No be wuna sabi da kain waka?
Na waka wey you di waka like sei
You get na mutoli, da sick wey
Oyibo dem di call'am hernia.
Na so waka for saggin' pants dei.

Taim wey prisoner pipo
Be commot for ngata,
Da mutoli waka dong ton be
Na dem own fashion!
You wan pass for any side,
You di daso nye 'prison graduate'
You di waka wit trosa for you dem shit hole.
Na so waka for saggin's pants dei.
For Kontri for Barack Obama,
waka for saggin's pants na helele!
Dis waka dong ton be na fashion!

Some Akata pipo,
Da mean sei:

Black pipo for America,
Dem di born pikin so dem go start for land dem
waka for saggin's pants taim wey
pikin di still drink boobie.
Oh yes, dis wan na turu turu tok!
No be da wan na development?

I dong look dis palava so,
I ton'am, ton'am for ma head,
I ton'am, ton'am,
I shake ma kongolibon head,
I sei "wonders shall never end in this wold!"
I dong tell ma own pikin dem sei:
'You shall wear this thing over my dead body!'
No be wuna sabi sei taim wey yi dong bad,
Repé di tok na gramma for tchotchoro?

Speak Camfranglais Pour Un Renouveau Ongolais

I will not parler français at home.
Je ne parlerai point French on the school grounds.
I will not speak French avec mes copains…
I will not speak French with mes camarades de classe…
I will not speak français tout court.
Hello! Ils ne sont pas bêtes, ces Anglos!
Après maintes reprises, ça commenc à pénétrer dans leurs têtes de cochon!

Dans n'importe quel esprit.
ça fait mal;
ça fait honte;
ça agace!
ça blesse!
Et on ne speak pas French dans les carabets de matango.
Ni dans les gares routières.
Ni anywhere else non plus.
On ne sait jamais avec ces conasses de froggies!
D'ailleurs, qui me donne cette autorité de crier à tue-tête?
D'écrire ces sacrées lignes?
Peu m'importe!

J'écrirai ce qui me chante.
Sous n'importe quel ciel,
ça laisse voir qu'on n'est rien que des Ongolais de souche.
Don't mind the frogs: if you are not heureux ici, allez ailleurs!
We're not tout simplement des conards, you know!
Zut alors! ça commence à me taper sur les nerfs.
J'appelle un chat un chat.

Faut dépasser ça, any how.
Faut parler camerounais.
Faut regarder la télévision en camerounais.
Faut écouter la radio in camerounais.
Comme tout bon Camer.
Why not just go ahead and learn English?
Don't fight it, vous pigez?

It's easier anyway.
No bilingual schools,
No bilingual constitutions,
No bilingual ballots,
No bilingual toll-gates,
No bilingual billboards,
No bilingual commercials,
No danger of internal frontiers!

Enseignez le camerounais aux enfants dès le bas âge.
On n'a pas réellement besoin de parler français quand même.
Do we really need English de toute façon?
L'Ongola c'est le L'Ongola, no be so?
Le chien aboie et la caravane passe, I di tell you!
On restera toujours rien que de sales conards
Si on continue à se casser la gueule à cause
Du patois de l'ex-colon.
Conards, Conasses? Non, non, ça gêne!
On n'aime pas ça. C'est pas cute!
ça nous fait bagarrer,
ça nous fait pleurnicher,
ça nous fait rire jaune,
Mais quand on doit rire ou pleurer,
C'est en quelle langua qu'on rit ou pleure?

Voyez-vous, we dei for véritable catch 22!

Ah, ah!

Et pour aimer?

Et pour haïr?

Et pour vivre…?

Schizophrénie Nationale

Comment peut-on être Camerounais ?
Le français est-elle ma langue maternelle ?
Non, je suis né à Abakwa où l'on ne le parle pas.
Comment peut-on être Camerounais ?
L'anglais est-elle ma langue maternelle ?
Non, je suis né à Bertoua où l'on ne le parle pas.
Suis-je même Camerounais ?
Vraiment, je le crois et m'en expliquerai
Mais de 'pure ethnie' qu'en sais-je et qu'importe ?
Ne m'insultez pas !
Séparatiste ? Autonomiste ? Régionaliste ?
Tout cela, rien de cela. Au-delà !
Mais alors, nous ne nous comprenons plus.

Qu'appelez-vous Camerounais ?
Et d'abord, pourquoi l'être?
Question nullement absurde.
Camerounais d'état-civil, je suis nommé Biafrais.
J'assume à chaque instant ma situation de Camerounais;
Mon appartenance au Cameroun,
N'est en revanche qu'une qualité facultative
Que je puis parfaitement renier ou méconnaître.
Je l'ai d'ailleurs fait ;
J'ai longtemps ignoré que je suis Camerounais.

Camerounais sans bagages,
Il me faut donc être Anglophone en surplus.
Camerounais sans ambages,
Il me faut donc être Francophone en plus.
Si je perds cette conscience,

L'appartenance cesse d'être en ma science.

Le Camerounais n'a pas de pièces d'identité,

Il n'existe que dans la mesure où,

A chaque génération,

Des hommes reconnaissent leur Camerounité.

A cette heure, des enfants naissent à Bamenda,

Seront-ils Camerounais ?

A cette heure, des enfants sont mis au monde à Bertoua,

Seront-ils Camerounais ? Nul ne le sait.

A chacun, l'âge venu, la découverte ou l'ignorance.

Bitter Kola

Noix de kola—
Véritable aprodisiaque africain!
Noix de kola—
Bête noire du 'viagra' hellène.
Noix de kola—
Bon compagnon de route!

Noix de kola—
Source intarissable d'énergie—
Energie pour faire la course;
Energie pour faire la promenade;
Energie pour faire la causerie;
Energie pour faire la bagarre;
Energie pour faire l'amour;
Energie pour se mettre au travail;
Energie pour se mettre à danser.
Noix de kola—
Vrai passe partout!

Bitter Kola—
Qui partage la kola,
Apporte la vie,
Vieil adage africain!

A La Manière des Saras

Je n'oublierai jamais
Ma première classe de français!
Je suis arrivé tôt dans la classe.
J'y suis entré et j'ai attendu patiemment
Le début des cours avec les autres.

J'étais fort nerveux.
Le professeur mince comme une baguette,
Avec la voix d'oiseau s'est mise à nous
Asseoir par ordre alphabétique.
Elle m'a appelé en dernier lieu
Et j'ai trouvé ma place.

A ce moment-là,
J'ai jeté un coup d'oeil sur
Une camarade metoch avec qui j'allais
Partager le banc pendant
Toute l'année scolaire.
Et mon coeur a commencé à
Battre plus vite que d'habitude.
Je n'oublierai jamais
Ce jour de baptême du feu
A la manière des nassara!

Hymne Camerien

Mes complices de Nkouloulou-o!
Ma complice dem for Nkouloulou-o!
Mes taras de Moloko-o!
Ma tara dem for Moloko-o!
Ma mombo dem for Marché central-o!
Mes amis du Marché central-o!
Ma kombi dem for Kumba market-o!
Mes potes au Marché de Kumba-o!
Ma dong pipo dem for Kasala farm-o!
Les sauveteurs du Mbanga-o!
De wan dem for Camp Sic de Bassa-o!
Ceux du Camp Sic de Yabassi-o!

Sep da wan dem for ngata for Tchollire-o!
Même ceux qui purgent des peines
Au sein de la prison de Tchollire-o!
De wan dem for Robben Island de Kondengui,
Ceux qui végètent dans la prison
Cauchemardesque de Kondengui
Ala wan em for prison de Mantoum-o!
Les autres en prison de Bamenda-o !
Sep da wan dem for Buea!

Laissez-moi vous langua cette nouvelle.
I sei mek I langua wuna dis tori.
Un nouvel hymne national vient de naître à Ongola.
Some national anthem dong commot
Just now for Ongola.
Da mean say some national anthem
Dong show head for we own kontri.

Voici comment se chante notre hymne national:

Le Cameroun c'est le cameroun,
On va faire comment alors?
That is to say,
Cameroon is Cameroon,
What can we do?
In ala word,
Cameroon na Cameroon,
We go do na how-no ?

Grand Katika d'Etoudi,
Kick all ndou for caisses de l'Etat,
On chante toujours:
Le Cameroun c'est le Cameroun,
On va faire comment alors ?
That is to say,
Cameroon is Cameroon,
What can we do?
In ala word,
Cameroon na Cameroon,
We go do na how-no ?

Les ministres détournent leurs mbourous de l'Etat,
On chante sans cesse:
Le Cameroun c'est le Cameroun,
On va faire comment alors ?
That is to say,
Cameroon is Cameroon,
What can we do?
In ala word,
Cameroon na Cameroon,

We go do na how-no ?

Les zangalewa matraquent
Les étudiants en grève sur le campus
De l'Université de Buea, jusqu'à les nyoxer,
On chante comme d'hatibude:
Le Cameroun c'est le Cameroun,
On va faire comment alors ?
That is to say,
Cameroon is Cameroon,
What can we do?
In ala word,
Cameroon na Cameroon,
We go do na how-no?

Les mange-mille meng les taximan
Parcqu'ils ont refusé de choko,
On chante seulement:
Le Camer c'est le Camer,
On va faire comment alors ?
That is to say,
Cameroon is Cameroon,
What can we do?
In ala word,
A Cameroonian is a Cameroonian,
We go do na how-no ?

Les gendarmes violent les bayam sellam
Parce qu'elles ne veulent pas donner le café,
On chante sans cesse:
Le Cameroun c'est le cameroun,
On va faire comment alors ?

59

That is to say,
Cameroon is Cameroon,
What can we do?
In ala word,
Cameroon na Cameroon,
We go do na how-no ?

Les hommes politiques
Truquent les élections à vue d'oeil,
Parce qu'ils sont affligés de la mégalomanie,
On chante:
L'Ongola c'est l'Ongola,
On va faire comment alors ?
That is to say,
Cameroon is Cameroon,
What can we do?
In ala word,
Cameroon na Cameroon,
We go do na how-no ?

Le gouvernement refuse de goudronner les routes,
Parce les ministres ont tout kick,
On chante sans avoir honte:
Le Cameroun c'est le cameroun,
On va faire comment alors ?
That is to say,
Cameroon is Cameroon,
What can we do?
In ala word,
Cameroon na Cameroon,
We go do na how-no ?

Les fonctionnaires sont compressés
A cause de la crise économique et la corruption endémique,
Engendrée par le dysfonctionnement étatique,
On chante:
Le Cameroun c'est le cameroun,
On va faire comment alors ?
That is to say,
Cameroon is Cameroon,
Na so da we own
Cameroon National Anthem dei!

What can we do?
In ala word,
Cameroon na Cameroon,
We go do na how-no ?
Na so da we own
Hymne ongolais dei!

Les diplômés d'université
Se retrouvent au Chomencam,
On chante comme des moutons:
Le Cameroun c'est le cameroun,
On va faire comment alors ?
That is to say,
Cameroon is Cameroon,
Na so da we own
Cameroon National Anthem dei!

Le Grand Katika nous largue
Une constitution constipée
Bekoz il veut crever au pouvoir,
On chante bêtement,

Pour ne pas dire moutonnement:
Le Cameroun c'est le cameroun,
On va faire comment alors ?
That is to say,
Cameroon is Cameroon,
Na so da we own
Cameroon National Anthem dei!

Les Mbere-Khaki meng
Des bendskinneurs foreska affaire nkap,
On chante:
Le Cameroun c'est le cameroun,
On va faire comment alors?
That is to say,
Cameroon is Cameroon,
Na so da we own
Cameroon National Anthem dei!

Le Chop Pipo Dem Moni party(CPDM)
Nous fait voir de toutes les couleurs,
Parce qu'il n'y a pas moyen
Pour les partis d'opposition ongolais d'y faire face,
On chante comme des cinglés:
Le Cameroun c'est le cameroun,
On va faire comment alors ?
That is to say,
Cameroon is Cameroon,
Na so da we own
Cameroon National Anthem dei!
Le Grand Katika sort tout l'argent
De la Caisse noire présidentielle
Afin d'aller construire

Son hôpital privé à Baden-Baden
On chante peureusement:
Le Cameroun c'est le cameroun,
On va faire comment alors ?
That is to say,
Cameroon is Cameroon,
Na so da we own
Cameroon National Anthem dei!

Une wolowoss se métamorphose en Première Dame
On chante:
Le Cameroun c'est le cameroun,
On va faire comment alors ?
That is to say,
Cameroon is Cameroon,
Na so da we own
Cameroon National Anthem dei!

Un professeur ongalais dépassé
Par l'état des choses s'écrie:
Vraiment le cameroun est formidable,
Vivons seulement.
Da mean sei:
Cameroon na wandaful
Mek we begin nye daso.
C'est le comble!

Glossaire

A

Aboki: ami, vendeur de soya
Achouka: bien fait pour toi!
Achouka ngongoli: bien fait pour toi!
Aff: affaire
Akwara: prostituée
Ala: autre
Allô: mensonge
A mort: tellement
Anglo: Anglophone au Cameroun.
Apprenti-sorcier: opposant
Ashawo: prostituée

B

Badluck: malchance
Bangala: pénis
Bao: grand
Barlok: malchance
Bled: maison, pays, village
Bolè: terminer, venir à terme, mourir
Bro: frère

C

Camer: camerounais
Camerien: camerounais
Capo: personne influente; directeur
Chaud gars: dragueur; Paul Biya
Chavoum: fusil
Check: penser; songer à
Chia: poste; siege

Chiba: acte de faire la chatte; parler des feymans
Chop chia: remplacer; succéder à
Close: habits, vêtements
Coma: cinema
Commot: s'en aller; sortir, avoir lieu ; venir de
Crish: fou, folle, saoul, saoule

D
Day: il y a
Dash: faire cadeau; donner
Dem: lutter ; se battre
Depuis from: Il y a longtemps
Djimtété: caid, chef de bande
Dos:l'argent, les sous
DSK: Dominique Strauss-Kahn

E
Ekié! interjection qui marque la surprise

F
Fais quoi, fais quoi: quoi qu'il arrive; coûte que coûte
Feyman: escroc
Fok: faire l'amour, baiser
Frog: Francophone au Cameroun

G
Gee: donner; céder à
Gombo: légume, affaire juteuse
Grand Camarade: El Hajj Ahmadou Ahidjo

H

Haba! Exclamation qui marque la surprise

Half-book: Analphabète

Homme Lion: Paul Biya, Président camerounais actuel

I

If: si

J

Jeune talent: Jeune homme, jeune fille,

Je wanda: je me demande

Jobajo: boisson alcoolique; bière

Johnny: marcher a pied; se promener

Johnny-Four-Foot: chèvre; imbécile

K

Kamambrou; chef d'état, dirigeant

Kam-no-go: maladie de la peau qui une fois déclenchée, ne finit pas

Kanda: la peau; parties sexuelles

Kan-kan: toutes sortes de; une variété de

Katika: patron; directeur

Kengué: Imbécile

Kick: voler, dérober

Kicker: voler, dérober

Kickman: voleur

Knack kanda: faire l'amour; baiser

Kolo: mille francs CFA

Kondre: pays

L

Langua: parler; langue; discours

L'homme Lion: Paul Biya

Long: maison; domicile

Lookot:faire attention

M

Mange-mille: policier

Manioc: vagin; parties privées de la femme

Massa: monsieur; patron

Matango: vin de palme

Mazembe: bandit

Mboa: pays

Mbom: mec, gars

Mbombo: homonyme

Mbourou: l'argent; les sous

Mbout: stupide; idiot

Mboutoucou: stupide; idiot

Mboutman: stupide; idiot

Meng: crever; mourir

Merco: Mercédès

Metoche: métisse

Mini minor: femme de petite taille

Mola: gars

Mougou: fainéant

Muna: bébé

N

Nassara: homme blanc

Nchinda: serviteur; subalterne

Ndamba: ballon; match de football

Ndiba: l'eau

Ndomo: frapper; se battre
Ndoutou: malchance
Nga: fille; femme
Ngata: prison
Ngataman: prisonnier
Ngola: Cameroun
Ngui: fille; femme
Nioxer: baiser; faire l'amour
Njoh: gratuit
Njoter: profiter
Nkane: prostituée
Nkap: l'argent, les sous
Ntamulung choir: bruit inutile
Ntong: la chance
Nyè: voir; jeter un coup d'oeil sur
Numéro six: sixième sens; intelligence

O
Odontol: boisson alcoolisée produit au Cameroun
Ongola: Cameroun
Ongolais: camerounais

P
Pa Pol: Paul Biya
Padre: Prêtre
Palava: affaire
Perika: Petit frère
Pipo: gens
Politiquart: politicien
Popol: Paul Biya; Président camerounais
Poum: s'enfuir; s'échapper

Q
Quat: quartier; pays, domicile

R
Radio trottoir: la rumeur; bruit
Rdépéciste: membre du Rassemblement Démocratique du Peuple Camerounais (RDPC); parti politique au pouvoir au Cameroun.
Refré: frère
Remé: mere
Repé: père

R
Sabi: savoir; connaître
Saper: s'habiller
Sara: homme blanc; femme blanche
Sharp sharp: de bonne heure; très tôt le matin
Sissia: menace; impressionner
Soya: viande de boeuf; pourboire
Squatter: rester; être domicilié à; demeurer

T
Tanap: se mettre debout
Tara: complice
Tchat: raconter; dire
Tchatcher: raconter; dire
Tchotchoro: gamin(e); adolescent(e)
Tchouquer: faire l'amour; baiser
Titi: nana; fille
Tok: parler; dire
Toli: fait divers

V
Villaconcon: villageois(e)

W
Wanda: s'étonner; se demander
Wok: travail; travailler
Wolowoss: prostituée

Y
Ya: écouter; entendre
Ya bad: souffrir
Yo: jeune gars très chic
Yoyette: jeune fille très chic; une chic fille

Z
Zangalewa: soldat; militaire